M000002981

PUBLISHED *by* PARABLES
Earthly Stories with a Heavenly Meaning

Grandmother's House

Grandmother's House

A Trilogy

By

Sara

(Child of God)

PUBLISHED by PARABLES
Earthly Stories with a Heavenly Meaning

Grandmother's House

Grandmother's House: A Trilogy
Sara (Child of God)

Published By Parables
September, 2020

ISBN 978-1-951497-81-1
Printed in the United States of America

Readers should be aware that Internet Web sites offered as citations and/or sources for further information may have been changed or disappeared between the time this was written and the time it is read.

GRANDMOTHER'S HOUSE

HOUSE

A TRILOGY

BY

SARA

(CHILD OF GOD)

PUBLISHED *by* PARABLES
Earthly Stories with a Heavenly Meaning

Grandmother's House

Disclaimer

Some may get offended by my stories.

If you do get offended, then this is not meant for you.

They are for the people who need to hear them and be encouraged by them -- to share their stories

You are not alone.

I am not a victim. I am Victorious!

'Hear me roar!'

Are you ready to tell your story?

Table of Contents:

A Trilogy

1

Grandmother's House

Grandmother's House

Page 1

My grandma's house is in one of the safest cities in America. Well, it was not a safe place for me.

<u>Page 2</u>

She was two different people. There was the nice daytime grandma, and at night there was the mean one. I got to know them both–especially the nighttime one.

Page 3

When I was a little girl, my mother, sister, and I slept over at her house.

Everything was fine during the day, but when darkness came, so did the trouble.

I was the chosen one, and this only happened to me.

When the moon came up, everything became cold.

Page 4

My family slept on the living room floor downstairs.
When night arrived, my grandma came out of her room
upstairs and went down to wake me up.

I was told to go upstairs and change and come back
down. I did as I was told.

When I returned, I was in a white dress; I was
sleepwalking into someone else's nightmare.

Page 5

She told me to drink some juice from a bottle which made my head go dizzy. I asked, "Grandma, what is this?" She told me it would make me relax and everything would be okay.

I was drifting in and out of reality. I didn't know what was real anymore. As I walked out of the door, I looked back knowing I would never be the same.

<u>Page 6</u>

I was transported into a car that was taken to another house. The house looked normal. Everything looked normal.

When I stepped into the house, I could hear eerie sounds. My body went completely numb. I immediately felt the presence of evil spirits everywhere.

Page 7

It was a house of terror. Atrocious things were being done. I was put in a small room waiting to be called.

I wasn't supposed to be here. I was crying and asking, "God, why is this happening to me?" I was knocking on the wall really hard but nobody heard me. Nobody came to rescue me. I was completely devastated.

Page 8

As I was crying, someone touched my shoulder. When I looked up, there was the most beautiful woman with long black shiny hair which covered her face. Her white gown sparkled in the light. She sang to me in her sweet voice which carried through the tiny room. She held me in her arms and told me everything would be okay. When she told me that, peace came into my heart.

Page 9

When I came back to my grandma's house, she told me
to change clothes and go back to sleep. She said not to
tell anybody because they wouldn't believe me. The next
day she pretended like it never happened, and that was
the worst.

Should I be angry, bitter, and betrayed? Yes, of course, these were all the feelings I felt and more. But should I be mad forever? No, because it was killing me! I was drinking my own poison. I did it the world's way and I only felt worse. I was depressed and nothing could help me. What helped me overcome this situation was JESUS.

I was a Christian all my life, but when I asked Jesus to be my Lord and Savior and let Him come into my heart, my whole life changed. My life didn't suddenly become easy, but I became free. I was not alone anymore.

"And you shall know the truth, and the truth shall make you free."

John 8:32 NKJV

My life verse is Jeremiah 29:11 NKJV

"For I know the thoughts that I think toward you, says the Lord, thoughts of peace and not of evil, to give you a future and a hope."

Even if your beginning wasn't good, your future is filled with hope that only God can give you. I know it is hard and it will take a while but it is so worth it.

There is a picture of Jesus hanging on my grandma's living room wall. When I look up at him, He is crying and I know He understands me.

My grandma fed me lies which I believed for a very long time. God has restored me so I can say now that I forgave her. And I keep forgiving her because forgiveness is not for her; it is for me. I give everything to God and let him run the show. When I go to her house, the picture of Jesus on the wall is smiling at me and I am smiling back.

I can now go visit my grandma and give her a hug. It feels good that I can be in the same room as her. I love her.

Let all bitterness, wrath, anger, clamor, and evil speaking be put away from you, with all malice. And be kind to one another, tenderhearted, forgiving one another, even as God in Christ **forgave you.**

Ephesians 4:31-32 NKJV

You can choose to be bitter or you can let go and choose Jesus

I chose Jesus! Who will you choose?

Grandmother's House

2

One Night in Jail

Grandmother's House

Grandmother's House

I wish my jail experience was like Peter and John praising Jesus all the night long. But, my story is a little bit different. You know when people tell you their "rock bottom story," well this is mine. I am not going to tell you what I went in for but let's just say I did something bad and if I told you, then I must kill you. Which will probably put me in jail again. It is not like what you see on TV or in the movies. This was not a Law & Order: Special Victims Unit Episode.

The worst part was being escorted to the police car handcuffed and put in the back of the car. That was a low point for me; I am a skinny girl with a skinny wrist. Oh boy, those were hard to take off. Believe me, I tried hard. When the policeman took the handcuffs off me, I couldn't feel my hands for a good two minutes, I thought my wrist was broken.

I get to the holding station and have my picture taken and then I'm fingerprinted. I did call and got the bail bond. There was a lot of waiting. Then afterward, I went back into the car handcuffed where they took me to a jail cell where I would be spending the night.

Grandmother's House

There was one jail toilet. The thick concrete beds were attached to the walls. The food sucked. Yelp I had a five-star experience. Also, I was not alone I had company.

I couldn't sleep at night especially with my jail mate masturbating.

It was horrible, I am not a criminal. I am a good girl. I don't belong here. I had so much time to think. I knew I didn't want to be here again. For that to happen, I knew I needed Jesus again because I couldn't do this myself. I spent one night in jail and that ruined me. I knew this will be a bigger problem if I didn't change immediately. This did not only affect me but my loved ones as well.

When I woke up the next day, the bail bond came through and I was released from jail. I was a different person. I knew what I did was wrong, and I decided to never do it again. I knew the process of change was not going to be easy. I needed to change the way I think and act. I surrounded myself with people who spoke life into me. I knew I can change and believed only God could do this in my life. He sure did!

The journey is not easy, but it is worth it. I went to church since I was a kid and I knew Jesus or at least I thought I did. I then fell away from Him. God met me where I was, also brought me to a church, put the right people in my life who loved me and who saw my potential even before I did.

I did counseling, took a recovery class, and a discipleship program.

There is freedom in Jesus. I once found identity in the world but now I know my identity is in Jesus Christ. I got out of the way and let God run the show.

Whether you knew Jesus as a Child like me or never stepped into a church. You hear stories of how people met Jesus in jail, through people or even visions. However, it happened, Jesus was there with you the whole time.

Your sin is not too big. You are not a lost cause. Jesus died for you and your sins. God loves you and is waiting for you.

There is freedom.

"Are you tired? Worn out? Burned out on religion? Come to me. Get away with me and you'll recover your life. I'll show you how to take a real rest. Walk with me and work with me—watch how I do it. Learn the unforced rhythms of grace. I won't lay anything heavy or ill-fitting on you. Keep Company with me and you'll learn to live freely and lightly."

Matthew 11:28-30 (The Message Bible)

3

It Starts with Forgiveness

Grandmother's House

Grandmother's House

Disclaimer: Some may get offended by my story. Please pray as you read this. Pray for people who are trafficked to become rescued, restored, and redeemed. Please pray for people who are in forced labor as well.

- Forgive others

- Forgive God

- Forgive yourself

Definition of human trafficking

Organized criminal activity in which human beings are treated as possessions to be controlled and exploited (as by being forced into prostitution or involuntary labor) Webster Dictionary.

Some of the things, I might say are going to be uncomfortable to hear. I understand this is a sensitive subject and I will handle everything with the utmost care.

I will be sharing some of what went on in the house of terrors. I will also, share with you on how I found closure and healing. How I am continuing on my road to recovery.

I was trafficked as a Child,

I was trafficked as a Child, however; I was also part of a satanic ritualistic ceremony. Yes, I was pimped out by my own grandmother and sold to the devil. I didn't know who I was, I was whoever everybody wanted me to be. I was lost but later I would be found.

I was very angry and I didn't know why. For, the longest time I thought this was someone else's nightmare that I was walking into. This was real life and I didn't know what to do. I thought why was this happening to me. I felt so alone.

Why did, my grandmother choose me and not my sister. Why was I the chosen one? All, these questions running through my mind.

This was hell on earth for me.

When I was at my grandmother's house I was told to go upstairs and wear a white dress and only the white dress. I was given some "juice" to drink as I was coming down the stairs, I knew something was not right. I walked out of my grandmother's house looking back at my mom and sister sleeping on the living room floor. As the door closed behind me, something in me closed as well.

I was dressed in white like a Child bride waiting. Just waiting to be told what to do. Every time, it was different.

When I walked into another person's house which I didn't recognize. I immediately felt coldness. You felt the presence of evil.

You were put in a small room

One thing I noticed was everything was organized. Everybody had a part to play and they did it well. The people looked normal. The people weren't creepy. They were just lifeless.

There were noises but I couldn't tell if it came from a human or animal. Maybe, it was both. Who knows?

There were strange symbols everywhere. There were candles and incenses perfectly placed. There was a lot of blood drinking. I didn't know if it came from an animal or human. Maybe, both. Every blood tasted different and had a different texture.

When you arrived you were put in a small room. Until you were called.

.

I was lost and lonely

The room was set-up like a Child bedroom filled with dolls and toys. There was also a video camera in the background recording the Children play. Back in the day, the video camera was big and bulky. The room reminded me of the training room in Disney's Pixar's Monsters Inc.

There was the upstairs room "The upper room."

This is where the "special people" were. This is where everybody wanted to be. You had to be chosen to go up there. I got chosen to participate in the activities upstairs. People will be surprised but it was not as kinky as people might think. It was more odd and strange.

It was very confusing

There were so much going on in the house. You felt like a caged animal most of the time. There were adults and Children. Yet, you couldn't converse with anybody.

There were people who I thought was nice but now I know were not. It was very confusing.

All, I wanted to do is go back home. Which, was grandmother's house.

Most, of the time I was in a small room locked up. I guess that was my first "jail" experience. I was banging on the wall for someone to help me but no one rescued me. I was lost and lonely.

Grandmother pretended…

As I went back to Grandmother's house, I felt numb. I was used and abused. The person who was supposed to take care of me and watch over me caused me the most pain. I didn't know who I was supposed to trust. I was violated and completely humiliated.

I woke up the next day, and my grandmother pretended it never happened.

Through counseling, I learned I was trafficked. I believed in the stereotypical definition thinking this happens overseas and not in the states.

She didn't go to jail.

The fear, depression, and anxiety stemmed from the root of my Childhood past. It carried into my adult life. I became an Angry Asian Woman. I hurt myself and others. I didn't like where this was heading.

I needed to forgive my grandma and everyone who had hurt me.
I knew the only way to heal was to forgive my grandmother. It was not for her but for me so I can be set free from the pain and move on. The anger was robbing my happiness. It was for me to move on with my life.

My grandmother didn't get punished. She didn't go to jail.

She said I was lying

Only one family member believes me.

I told my immediate family what happened to me a long time ago.

I would do a one on one and family group confrontation, but nobody believed me.

I did have a one on one confrontation with my grandmother in the kitchen.
I asked her about what happened in the past. She denied it. She said I was lying.

Was that enough for me? No.
I knew her answer would be different when there was a group confrontation in front of the family. I was right.

I needed this for me. I was not looking for forgiveness. I was breaking a family generation curse. I was voicing the truth.

For me, I needed to confront my accuser. I did mine in a public setting. It is not for everybody. Make sure whatever you do, you feel comfortable.

An awkward, icy laugh.

I did confront my grandmother and my whole family. Coming into it, I knew she was not going to acknowledge the situation and ask for forgiveness. I did bring a married couple to facilitate the whole thing but also to be my witnesses as well. Nobody believed me.

My grandmother let out a laugh. It was an awkward and icy laugh.

The thing is she did not confirm or deny my claims. Someone else in the room defended her.

After the confrontation, nobody mentioned this again. Afterward, I talked it over briefly with my immediate family. None of my extended family members reached out to me afterward.

What happened to me was wrong and a crime. I was raped and sexually assaulted.

I needed to get this off my chest. I just needed to say this to me, for me. I was not looking for an apology. I did my closure in this matter.

A long recovery process

For, the longest time I didn't go to my grandmother's house. I can now go up to my grandma and hug her. I can be in the same room with her. This is huge for me.

There is still the same picture of Jesus hanging on the living room wall in my grandmother's home today, the same picture I passed by as a little girl, however, this time around Jesus is smiling at me and I am smiling right back at him.

It was a long recovery process and still today I am learning to recover and heal.

What happened to me was not my fault. This was a big lesson for me to learn. For me to move on I needed to let go and give everything to God. Everybody's recovery looks different.

I need Jesus and I am learning to have a better relationship with him. God has sent me wonderful people into my life. There were people who believed in me and saw something great in me. When I didn't even see that in myself.

I still love her and forgive her.

Forgiveness is not a one-time deal. I wish it was! I have to keep on forgiving my grandmother.

I still love her and forgive her.

I am working on my boundaries and being balanced. Thank you to all the people who have helped me in my recovery process and who will help with my continued transformation.

For my future ministry, I will work with anti-human trafficking organizations to help people be set free and restored. I want to focus on people who have been trafficked in the states. This is my life ministry.

I am a trafficked survivor.

Slavery is a state of mind!

I choose to be free!

I am a trafficked survivor.

This is my story. My story points back to Jesus.

What is your story?

Forgiving others is a gift to yourself,
given not because the other deserves pardon,
but because you deserve the serenity and joy
that comes from releasing resentment and anger,
and from embracing universal forgiveness.

     –   Jonathan Lockwood Huie

Grandmother's House

Grandmother's House

CPSIA information can be obtained
at www.ICGtesting.com
Printed in the USA
BVHW020543261020
591803BV00001B/7